Rob Mack
Illustrations by Marižan

The New Mouse House

Bumblebee Books
London

BUMBLEBEE PAPERBACK EDITION

Copyright © Rob Mack 2021
Illustrations by Marižan

A CIP catalogue record for this title is
available from the British Library.

ISBN: 978-1-83934-094-9

Bumblebee Books is an imprint of
Olympia Publishers.

First Published in 2021

Bumblebee Books
Tallis House
2 Tallis Street
London
EC4Y 0AB

Printed in Great Britain

www.olympiapublishers.com

Dedication

To Cynthia Dawn, Andrew James, and Isobel Ruthe, who early in life became experts at moving to new houses

"The time is now," said Mrs. Mouse,
"To move us to another house
A house that stays dry in the rain,
April mop ups, what a pain!"

"Or bakes us out till we turn brown
When in July the sun burns down.
December we should all be cozy,
By our fire glowing rosy."

"North September winds are dreary,
Howling at our front door, 'Dearie!'
Close that door or from that rain
I fear we'll have to mop again!"

So everything was packed away,
This was to be their moving day.
All day their friends kept dropping by
To say farewell, sometimes to cry.

They said, "Goodbye." Maw swept the floor,
One last quick look and out the door.
The rain let up the sun came out
It's days like this you want to shout!

Each bigger mouse had one small pack,
Paw led the way along a track.
Maw with the babes took up the rear,
The bigger mice all stayed quite near.

Morning seemed so very long
Like miles and miles they had gone.
Along the river, past some hills
They paused beside some daffodils.

A little snack of bread and cheese
The bigger ones said, "Thanks and please."
Dishes washed and packed again,
Paw said, "Oh my, it looks like rain!"

So off they marched towards the west,
Those tired mice sure did their best.
Until the raindrops started down
Making puddles on the ground.

All rushed beneath a sturdy tree.
Paw said, "Well now this looks to be
the perfect place for us to stay
Until this rain has passed away."

"But night is near so let us sleep
Here all together, but no peep
Or rustling must be heard all night,
My tired mice, you'll all sleep tight."

"Oh Paw, oh Maw please let us stay
It's perfect for our house, oh may
We please live here? It looks like fun
With lots of room for us to run."

Maw said, "Perhaps, well I don't know."
Paw said, "I fear it won't be so.
An owl lives here in this tree."
And Maw just said, "I quite agree!"

All night the quiet mice slept sound,
The owl closely watched the ground.
But did not see and could not hear
Or know that tasty snacks slept near.

Next morning early, all was packed
And after tasty drinks and snacks.
They sneaked away towards the west
Passing by a robin's nest.

Through weeds along the river's mouth,
They travelled west and slightly south.
At noon they gathered in a bunch
And in a meadow ate their lunch.

The little ones all finished up,
Each had one berry in a cup.
While they played a quiet game
Maw and Paw called each by name.

Said Paw, "We must go to explore
We need you all to say no more.
Play quiet, while the babes both sleep.
Stay very close, don't make a peep."

"We want to come!" but Maw said, "No,
We two must hurry off now, so,
Behave and time will quickly pass!"
Then off they hurried, through the grass.

The babes slept sound, while bigger mice
Played a game with five small dice.
Maw and Paw soon came in sight,
So pleased to see no mousey fight.

"I've news," said Paw, "you all should hear.
Our brand new home is very near
Just to the south, we've found a spot
To build our house, a nice big plot."

Each mouse was happy as they packed
And fell in line behind Paw's back.
Beside a patch of purple clover,
Each mouse knew the search was over!

For the roof, a big grey rock
And little stones to line the walk
Lots of twigs for shiny floors,
For framing windows and for doors.

Maw and Paw worked very hard.
The babes played nicely in the yard.
The older mice both lent a paw,
Moving dirt and helping Maw.

One week later who'd have guessed,
This very cozy mice's nest
Is still so new, you'd swear they've been
Here all their lives, just like a dream!

All the family loves this house.
There are new friends for each small mouse,
For each a bedroom all their own,
Except the babes, until they've grown.

The fire every night glows bright
As Maw and Paw turn down the lights.
Each little mouse gets hugged and kissed
Then tucked in tight, no one gets missed.

Sometimes they miss the older place
And cry in bed, it's no disgrace
But now they're home and Maw says, "Soon
We'll holiday back there next June."

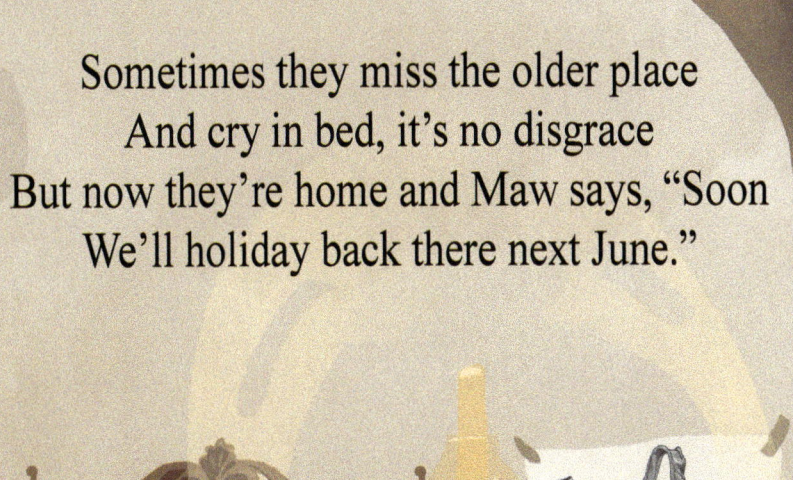

About the Author

Rob Mack is a father and grandfather who loves writing and telling stories at bedtime, in the morning, before and after supper, or any other time. As a young adult he earned a bachelor's degree in English Composition. This led to many years of work as a technical writer with opportunities to teach college courses in remote areas in Western Canada. He has always enjoyed writing stories for children from the experiences of children he knows and those he meets. As he travels to work in these remote areas, he loves to drop into local schools and tell stories where other storytellers never go.

He believes the best stories are about solving problems that are scary and learning how to become better creatures. Moving to a new house in another community is something that is sometimes scary for boys and girls as well as adults. Learning how to move by reading of the adventures of others, even mice, can help to make a scary time into an adventure.

Rob lives in Alberta, Canada with Mrs. Mack and 2 Siamese cats, Hector and Athena. In his spare time, he likes to solve problems by building things, traveling the world and having adventures.

About the Illustrator

Marižan (Maja Ranisavljev) is a theatre costume designer and an illustrator who enjoys creating for those who cherish the imaginative playful spirit.

She had first started a career as an illustrator for archaeological sites, and later drew sketches based on ancient treasure that could be found in the soil. Later, she drew inspiration in working with children's theatre and puppetry companies.

In her works she discovered that when telling a story using a child's voice and perspective, an adult was more immersed, and as though by magic paid more attention, while learning important lessons. Even today she recalls the scenes from her childhood and recreates the fragments of places and people and applies it in her work.

Growing up and being raised in the countryside her favorite place is the garden. She enjoys gardening and is constantly learning about growing plants from her mother, during visits to her parents' home.

She is an ardent observer of the secret life of her cats and other animals that live on the property. She is currently living in Pančevo, a town, in Serbia, with her family in a home full of books, plants, and toys.

And she hopes to always have one pet more.

CPSIA information can be obtained
at www.ICGtesting.com
Printed in the USA
BVHW062234020622
638582BV00004B/67